MW01615555

Ordering information: All Books published by CreativeU can be ordered by calling 949-716-9267 or via the Website at www.creativeu.com

ISBN: 0-9729877-4-6

Master Coach Series
Volume 3

Masterful Questions

Getting to the Heart of the Matter

By Michael Stratford MCC

"Supporting Coaches to Achieve Masterful Coaching"

"Supporting Clients to Achieve Masterful Lives"

Acknowledgments

There is a long list of people to whom I am grateful. Many of them have been clients, and many are fellow coaches. For those of you who aren't listed, simply know that I know who you are, and I appreciate your contribution to me becoming who I am.

This book grew out of curiosity. What book about questions wouldn't? The curiosity has always been mine, a curiosity for how the world works, and in particular how people work. This investigation is both strange and wonderful and has grown me a lot.

The demand was to produce material for a workshop to train coaches. Given that I have a "thing" about not showing up to lead a workshop without content, the material was easy to come up with, and here it is.

First and foremost I'd like to thank my incredible wife, Carly Anderson. She is a masterful coach in her own right. Her sense of what's readable has been a gift.

The person who is most responsible in this whole process is Jay Perry, my longtime coach, and even longer time friend. He has provided wisdom, humor, patience (god knows he needed it at times to coach me), and a constant unwavering belief in me.

I wish to also thank Deb Giffen, my longtime partner in creation of material for training coaches. She is truly a gifted coach but more importantly a champion for potential of the human spirit. She believes in me unquestioningly. This is a truly remarkable gift.

I am grateful for Sheila Kutner, my first business partner who gave me the experience of collaboration founded in love and appreciation for another's differences. She is an amazing coach, and a more amazing woman.

While I would like to thank all of the teachers I've had, a few stand out in particular: Bonnie Cogbill for believing in my acting talent and my ability to "become something." She was first in this list. Dan Fauci for challenging me to go beyond my beliefs to think for myself. Though I didn't always appreciate his methods, I am grateful for the stretch. Thomas Leonard for the uncommon vision to foster a profession where you can truly "have it your way," and to all the Teleclass Leaders, Colleagues and Friends at Coach U/Corporate Coach U/CCI and Comprehensive Coaching U who trained me and contributed to my evolution as a coach.

I'd like to thank Ken Abrams as a personal advocate extraordinaire. He is the supreme example of giving regardless of getting back. His clients are blessed to have him.

And lastly, I want to thank my father who has been deceased for some time. He taught me that anything is possible. Not by what he said, but by what he did. And I've never forgotten it.

In the words of Shakespeare, one of my favorite writers, and a wordsmith of uncommon means,

"I have no other words but thanks, thanks and ever thanks."

Welcome

Hi there,

Welcome to The Master Coach Series. This series of mini-books is designed to help you as a coach move toward Mastery in your profession...mastery of the skills, concepts and tools that make a great coach. This particular book is focused on Masterful Questions.

Over the course of the next ninety pages or so, we'll be working from our own question. It will be an inquiry into "What Makes Masterful Questions?" As part of the adventure, we will travel through a number of interesting lands, and even do a time shift. So, I hope you'll join me in a discovery process to simply see where it takes us all.

To repeat and paraphrase and oft used maxim, "If we go where we already know to go, we'll see what we've already seen, and learn what we've already learned." With that in mind we may wander a bit. On the following page is a map of sorts, so you can visit the land you would like to whenever in the order you'd like. That way, you create your own adventure as you encounter the different features of the landscape.

Since this is a primary skill set for coaches, I've included plenty of ways to practice getting at the heart of masterful questions. I urge you to try to do as many as possible to gain this mastery.

Have a great time, and by the way, I might ask you before you start out...What would be the most important thing you could gain from encountering this book? How would it aid you in your own journey toward mastery as a coach?

Yup, that's a sneaky way on my part to have you create an intention that will keep you focused while you read.

So, bye for now, and I'll see you back at the Inn.

Sincerely,

Michael Stratford, MCC

PS. At the back of the book is a request, an offer, and a shameless piece of promotion. Stop by if you're interested.

Captains Log

The Peak of Curiosity

All through our lives we've been taught to ask questions. Mostly though, we've been taught to ask questions for a singular distinct purpose. To find an answer, or in some cases "the" answer. We've forgotten that we were born to ask questions as part of our relationship and connection with the world. In some cases, a simple understanding of how things function, but in others, we may be asking deeper questions such as, "What the heck am I here for anyway?"

As children, we were born "not knowing." Right now I'm seriously delighted and amused at how much material is out in the world in books, tapes and seminars or workshops on getting to the state of "not knowing" as a desired place of "zen" living. This is not something that is new to us. We were born in this state. What has happened is that we've forgotten the joy, innocence and value of being there. Or worse, someone has beaten it out of us via schooling, work, or parental incursion as if to say...."Innocence and not knowing are a crime and need to be expunged, if you're going to be safe in the world...you must KNOW." What a silly way to live our lives. To indict the very beginnings of our lives as somehow inadequate to survive in the "real" world.

Children are curious about many things. They allow this natural curiosity to live joyously inside them and without discrimination. It's their method of finding their way in the world...i.e. "What are these things in my hand and how does it fit with me or I fit with it?" Their curiosity is free. Then, somewhere along the line there is a palace coup, and our parents, teachers, employers and sometimes our friends are part of it and the question is replaced by the Answer as King.

We get measured, tested, evaluated on answers and are rewarded or punished according to the requirement of how well our answer fits our question. We lost the joy of asking simply to find out what may be there. We have lost the pure curiosity that lives inside us and replaced it with a more purposeful curiosity, one that allows for some wandering, but very little wondering.

For coaches, the muscle of curiosity is essential. It's not sufficient if we're looking to help our clients achieve long term results and true evolution, it's not sufficient to just ask questions that will "solve the problem." Being curious about our clients situation is only the first level. In some circles it's called being curious about the "what" of our client.

It's important to be curious about who our clients truly are inside; what's really important to them and how this situation fits into the bigger picture of their entire life is a second level of curiosity. It's founded in the recognition that while the "what" of one's life is important (meaning the circumstances, the events, choices and decisions) it's really who they are in what they do, that really makes the difference. How's that for a jargon laden sentence?

The View from Mount Context

This is the framework that the coach asks questions from or through. The assumptions that one carries with them into a conversation will determine the basis for the questions they ask. For example: If a parent assumes the child has been misbehaving at school, and that their job as a parent is to keep the child in line, then their questions will have that particular flavor or "edge" to them.

They might not be interested in finding out what really happened, their questions might be more along the line of finding out what the child did wrong, how they intend to fix it, and most of all, "Will you ever do that again?"

In the meantime the child will sense the inherent accusation in the question as it approaches and most often, look to deflect blame away from themselves, or justify the choices he/she made by giving what seems to them a valid reason for their behavior…"But Billy punched me first…"

What hasn't happened is that the parent hasn't been curious enough to hear how the child sees the situation, what the child feels was the appropriate response and when discovering that, the parent hasn't then sought to find out from the child how the child thinks their behavior matches what works in the world…etc. There is an entire panoply of things not discussed, asked, or developed in that moment that will ultimately result in similar behavior in the child since there was taking advantage of the "developmental opportunity" , nor was there any honoring of the child's unique way to solve the situation that would ultimately be much easier for the child to maintain. So the questions come down to…

What is coaching really about?
What is the job of the coach?

This framework is often seen through the eyes of the assumptions that a coach views the client through. He then asks questions that are birthed from these lens. Let's see which assumptions are useful for the coach, and which get in the way of Masterful Questions.

The Plains of Respectful Assumptions

Here is a list of assumptions I've found to assist my ability to generate questions that make a difference. As you read them, please fill in what you find might be valuable in viewing the client from this vantage point. My own personal set of reasons is in the back of the book. How many of these are also yours?

A. The client is unique.

_____

_____

B. The client is intelligent.

_____

_____

C. The client is capable.

_____

_____

D. The client knows how to solve problems.

_____

_____

E. The client is responsible for his/her own life.

_____

_____

F. The client is an adult.

_____

_____

G. The client is personally accountable.

_____

_____

H. The client is imaginative.

_____

_____

I. The client is creative.

_____

_____

J. The client is courageous.

_____

_____

K. The client knows how to follow through.

_____

_____

L. The client has his/her own sense of order
and organizing principles.

_____

_____

M. The client has a unique dream/vision or goal.

_____

_____

N. The client has strengths, talents, and skills.

_____

_____

O. The client knows how to accomplish.

_____

_____

P. The client has or can get what they need.

_____

_____

Q. The client knows how to learn.

_____

_____

R. The client is whole.

_____

_____

S. The client knows how to be clear.

_____

_____

T. The client is resilient.

_____

_____

U. The client is competent in the world.

_____

_____

V. The client can provide for themselves.

_____

_____

W. The client knows how to focus.

_____

_____

X. The client has values and principles.

_____

_____

_____

Y. The client has their own inner compass.

_____

_____

_____

Z. The client is strong.

_____

_____

_____

And the last and most important…

The client is the expert on themselves.

_____

_____

_____

_____

_____

_____

In the last 8 yrs. as a coach, having logged over 10,000 hours of practice, these assumptions have served me well. Even when the client doesn't know he knows, or she doesn't trust her own wisdom, or know how to optimize the value of his/her strengths, talents or skills, all those things are still present.

Those items may be obscured, lost touch with, or even disowned, dismissed or distrusted. It still means to me that they are there, and they are worth honoring. Without being willing to honor those attributes in a client, we are sending a very subtle subliminal message in relating with them. We are sending the message that they are:
- Not good enough
- Can't trust themselves, their thoughts, or their actions

- Are incapable, incompetent or ignorant
- Are fragile and potentially helpless

Perhaps the most damaging message a coach can give...

"They need me for their success or they won't make it."

While there are many assumptions that help a coach approach a coaching session in a helpful fashion, there are also assumptions that are not helpful. On the next page is a list of assumptions by the coach that will create interference in the coaching relationship. Below each assumption, fill in how you think this assumption could create a roadblock for the coach.

PS...I'm aware you may disagree with some of these, but play along anyway, just for the sake of inquiry.

The Desert of Disempowerment

These assumptions will have a disempowering effect on either coach or client.

a. I have to be brilliant.

_____
_____
_____

b. My clients need me to hold them accountable

_____
_____
_____

c. Coaching is about getting results

_____
_____
_____

d. If my client isn't getting results I'm doing something wrong.

_____
_____
_____

e. My client is too fragile or delicate to handle the truth.

_____
_____
_____

f. I don't have expertise in that area so I can't coach them.

_____
_____
_____

g. My problem solving ability will come in handy for solving my client's problems.

_____
_____
_____

h. I give great advice.

_____

_____

i. I have X years experience in that field so I know what I'm talking about.

_____

_____

j. I have to come up with the right question at the right time.

_____

_____

k. Coaching is about telling people what they need to do.

_____

_____

l. A client's resistance to my suggestions indicates they are not committed.

_____

_____

m. The clients need me.

_____

_____

n. There is a right way for them to succeed.

_____

_____

o. If they're not doing the fieldwork, they have a fear of success.

_____

_____

p. My way is the way to do things.

_____

_____

_____

q. Every session must resolve the issue.

_____

_____

_____

r. Coaching is about solving problems.

_____

_____

_____

s. I have to get coaching right or it won't work.

_____

_____

_____

t. I don't need any training.

_____

_____

_____

u. I already know how to do "active listening."

_____

_____

_____

v. Training my skills will get in the way of my intuition.

_____

_____

_____

w. If one wants to succeed in life there are rules they have
   to follow.

_____

_____

_____

x. The client must be responsible in their life for the things they have or they'll never progress.

_____

_____

_____

y. Experience is the best teacher, and I have lots, so they should listen to me.

_____

_____

_____

z. My clients expect me to have the answers.

_____

_____

_____

aa. I've been coaching all my life.

_____

_____

_____

Had enough? Good.

The next part of context is what the job of coaching is about. The following pages give you an idea of the most powerful places a coach can work. If we are going to use masterful questions, we need to know what the job is. Ideally, we are working in two different places while simultaneously honoring both.

Whoville and Whatland

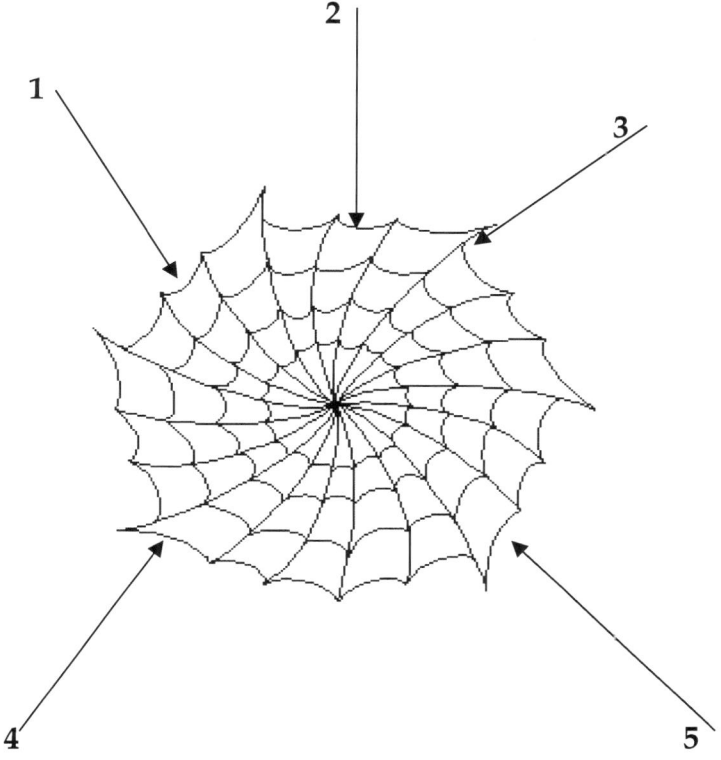

If we coaches, see our job as solving a client's problem or challenge, essentially we are working on one thread of the spider web of their life. This is what's called "focusing on the 'what'." While this may bring the interim satisfaction of an achieved result, the client has not necessarily grown in their ability to handle challenges in general, nor have they evolved their ability to create fewer challenges in their life. They've simply gotten a problem solved.

The trouble with this is that the client, like many an industrious spider, has many, many, many, threads in their web. Plus, they are constantly weaving more just in the process of life. The coaching process would become one problem-solving exercise after another until either the coach or the client (or both) get tired of the game and the relationship ends. That would leave the client with the experience of having solved lots of problems, but not necessarily having advanced in their life. Both they and the coach might feel the momentary sense of achievement that would eventually become hollowed out by the absence of personal evolution.

This would make the profession of coaching a short- term fix proposition. Given that there are any number of how-to-make-your-life-great-just-add-water systems and programs out there that would seem to address the same issues, there's not much point in having coaching be just one more of those. Since most of the programs that do not address integration of 'being' along with skills and development, eventually end up with the client pretty much back where they started. They may also be minus some money and time.

Coaching is so much more than that. It is the opportunity to address an individual situation while keeping an eye out for how the solution interacts with the bigger picture of their life. It is the opportunity to not only solve a problem, but also to shift how the person interacts with the world to either create fewer problems in general, or to draw fewer to them. It is the opportunity to go past the typical endpoint of "getting my life to work the way I want it to," and moving it to another level completely called "now that my life is pretty much working the way I want it to fairly consistently, what do I want to have my life be about?"

The latter is a much bigger question. It is in that question where legacy lives. It's what people want to leave as a representation of their time here in the world, or their contribution to the world while they are here.

None of these opportunities are available if the job of the coach is seen as "how do I fix this client's problem right now?"

What if, instead of simply addressing a single thread, the coach listens deeply, connects to the client, and asks questions that resonate in the core of the client or the center of the web? This can be done all the while paying attention to how this situation the client is currently facing, is related to who they are in the center of themselves and how this situation figures into the bigger picture of their whole life. It includes not only where they are now, but also where they want to go, and who they want to be when they get there.

This is called "coaching the who."

Let's look at the spider web again.

Coaching the Who is like coaching the spider in the center of the web. When a significant shift occurs in the center of the web (the center of the client), then the effects ripple out through every thread they encounter. Every decision, every challenge, every choice, or every opportunity is affected by what goes on in the center. In addition, because it is in the center and rippling out, it also affects every new thread the spider makes.

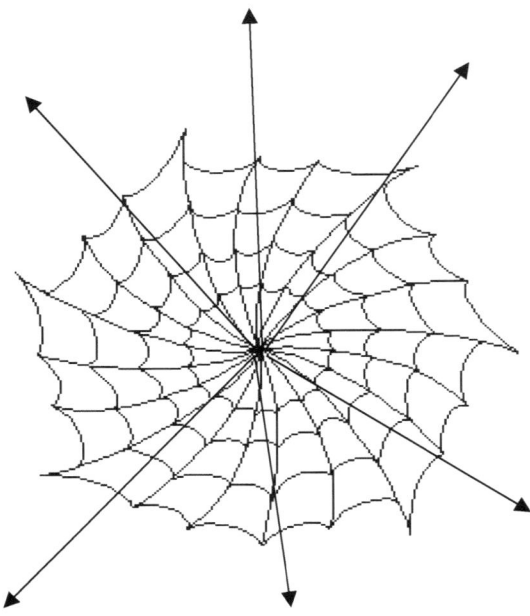

While there is immediate gratification in working with what's going on for a client, the presenting situation, the greatest and most long-lasting work comes from working on who they are. Ideally we can do both at the same time.

Below is an example of how the "who" affects the "what" of a client's actions in a real way.

Suppose…
One leader (A) of a business team is a person who believes in control. It's their belief that people need to know only what he determines they need to know in order to get the job done.

One leader (B) of a business team is a person who loves to develop other people into leaders. He believes that the inherent potential in people is extraordinarily valuable.

When team leader A interacts with his team, most likely you will witness this kind of behavior. The leader cuts off questions he deems irrelevant, or challenging to his authority. He gives people the minimal of information he thinks will get the job done. He will not want to waste time on others seeking to gather more information and would rather they just "do it." Productivity is his God.

When team leader B interacts with his team, most likely you will see something like this. The leader listens to questions to see what the opportunity is for this person to be developed into a more powerful leader herself. He might be more open to a process- oriented discussion and a certain amount of wandering in the discussion since he would rather they all learn than simply just "get to it." He will look for opportunities to allow others to lead and support them when they do. This person has the human- potential in people, being actualized as his God.

Both will achieve results. The results will be different in both cases. The team will grow or not grow in different directions. And productivity will occur either way. What will happen will be determined by the interaction, but what will not happen will also be determined by the interaction. It has been a question of who the team leader is in the business meeting that will have made the difference. Even if Team leader A pays lip service to the idea of developing other leaders because it is good management technique, the results will be different.

This fundamental difference is the key to coaches helping our clients evolve and therefore exhibit long term sustainable change vs. our clients simply solving a problem and then having to face another and another and another since the person who keeps generating these problems is themselves and their own ability to make a choice or decision.

A coach uses the questioning process to help with the main agenda, which is: "The client does the work." This way the client discovers, provides their own answers vs. the coach providing their answers for the client. Yes, the coach may have "right" answers for the client like a department store will have clothes that fit many people. The true value of coaching is in the client "owning" their solutions by discovering them. The result is a much truer "fit", not unlike having clothes tailor made for them instead of buying off the rack. In addition, many of the actions the client now chooses to take will come from their own set of possibilities rather than the coach's, and they will therefore, engender much less resistance to those choices.

Questions work in tandem with listening to provide the bulk of the coaching session. Linked with the context for coaching, is what coaches listen for, and how that adds to their ability to generate questions that are effective.

Listening deeply is where all great questions come from. However, much like the context of Coaching, it's what the coach is listening for, that makes the difference. This is linked to how the coach sees the client and the assumptions that a coach makes.

The two listening questions are:

What do people listen for?
What does a coach listen for?

The Forest of Listening

One of the chief impediments to being able to hear the questions our clients need us to ask comes from where we listen. Much like the contextual assumptions, there are useful places to listen from and not so useful places to listen from. In our journey throughout the world one of the creatures we will encounter is the W.O.L.F. which means, What One Listens For. The next chapter in the Captains Log describes the encounter with the Wolf and what to do about it.

Day 1: Discovering the W.O.L.F.

Listening is a skill we use hundred, or even thousands of times every day, yet for most of us it's an unconscious process. Although we hear and understand a lot of information, we haven't stopped to look at how the process of listening actually works.

We don't have a clue about why some things tend to stick in our memory and other things go "in one ear and out the other." We're not aware of what really motivates us to listen, and how our individual paradigms determine what we hear.

For example, take the simple statement: "I saw my mother today, and I gave her a big bouquet of flowers." Imagine how a mother might hear that statement. Now imagine how a therapist might hear that statement. Next, imagine how a florist might hear the statement; or a person whose mother had just died. Imagine a truck driver...a kindergarten student...a Hell's Angel...or a high-powered CEO. All of them would hear that same statement differently.

Each of us listens with an agenda that's based on the essence of who we are. We call this agenda our W.O.L.F. because it determines "What One Listens For." Our W.O.L.F. agenda is formed by our unique background and experiences. It's driven by either our conscious intentions or our unconscious hungers; sometimes even both. A coach's job is to be able to separate themselves from the Hunger-generated listening (The W.O.L.F.) that most people have and the more powerful listening appropriate to a coach.

In this section, we'll explore:

- How to deepen your listening skills
- How to discover the hungers that drive your listening
- How to get your hungers met so you don't "listen on an empty stomach"
- How to tame the W.O.L.F. (What One Listens For)
- What a masterful coach does and doesn't listen for
- How to listen to yourself
- How to use your natural listening strengths as a coach

W.O.L.F.

Although each of us has our own unique listening agenda, these agendas often fall into typical patterns. Recognizing your patterns, although not always comfortable, is the first step toward becoming an excellent listener, and a Masterful Coach. Review the list below and place a check mark by the listening pattern(s) that describe what you typically listen for.

- An opportunity to contribute

- A chance to make a point

- A place to say "See, I'm right!"

- A place to create affinity; "I know, I've been through the same thing!"

- A place to fix or solve the problem

- The moment where we may have to defend ourselves

Coaching Tip:
No one is immune to W.O.L.F. so you might as well get over it and "fess up". The sooner you do, the sooner you can begin to do something about it.

- An opportunity to show we care

- A place to put forth a belief or teach a lesson

- A chance to change the subject or make a joke

- A chance to join the conversation; to participate or belong

- A chance to gracefully exit

- A chance to distinguish ourselves or prove that we're different

- A chance to promote ourselves or prove that we're better

- An opportunity to correct

- Clues that show that we are "good enough"

- Signs that prove the other person likes us

The Hungers Behind the Wolf's Agenda

Behind each of the WOLF listening agendas is a hunger that needs to be fed. It could be a hunger for recognition, appreciation or attention…a hunger to be right, or to give or to instruct. Whatever the hunger, one thing always rings true. You can't ignore it. Like any hunger, you've got to recognize it and feed it if you want to release yourself from its grip.

Think back to your school days. Remember the last few minutes before lunch, and how hard it was to pay attention while your stomach was rumbling? Listening when you were physically hungry was very difficult, but it's an even bigger challenge to listen when you're hungry emotionally.

On the next page is a duplicate list of the 3 common emotional hunger types that keep us from being fully present while we listen. Take a moment to look through the list and see which hungers might be behind each of the W.O.L.F Listening Agendas. Add your insights to the "Hungers" column of the chart of Hungers and W.O.L.F. agenda. Then use your insights as you listen to your clients, your colleagues and yourself to see how these hungers influence a person's ability to "hear."

Coaching Tips:
Remembering to hold a context that a hunger is not a "bad" thing to have, it is simply what is…will keep you coaching from a space

Hungers

	Internal State	
<u>Inner-Directed</u>		<u>Outer-Directed</u>
To Receive	To Feel	Be/Have/Do
Receive Attention	Feel Important	Be Successful
Receive Love	Feel Secure	Be in Control
Receive Admiration	Feel Unrestricted	Be Right
Receive Respect	Feel Included	Have Power
Receive Acceptance	Feel Valuable	Be a Leader
Receive Recognition	Feel Needed	Be Useful
Receive Appreciation	Feel Safe	Be Cool

Receive Praise	Feel Loved	Teach Inform
Receive Credit-Thanks	Feel Connected	Achieve Accomplish
Receive Compliments	Feel Heard	Maintain Order
Receive Care	Feel Whole	Give to Others
Receive Support	Feel Complete	Be Perfect
Receive Gifts	Feel Excited	Be Responsible
Receive Touch	Feel at Peace	Be Creative
Receive Information	Feel Inspired	Be Consistent
Receive Help	Feel Honored	Be Unique
Receive Loyalty	Feel Clarity/Certainty	Get Results

W.O.L.F. Agenda	Hunger
An opportunity to contribute	
A chance to make a point	
A place to say, "See, I'm right!"	
A place to connect; "I've been through the same thing!"	
A place to fix or solve the problem	
The moment where we may have to defend ourselves	
To show we care	
A place to put forth a belief or teach a lesson	
A chance to change the subject	
A chance to join the conversation	
A chance to gracefully exit	
A chance prove that we're different	

Exercise

1. List your 3 main Listening Agendas:

a. _____

b. _____

c. _____

2. What are the Hungers behind each agenda?

a. _____

b. _____

c. _____

3. How might you get each of these Hungers met outside of the coaching relationship?

a. _____

b. _____

c. _____

4. Actively listen to the conversations around you, and practice identifying the Listening Agendas of the people you're speaking with. What do you notice about the different agendas? Where do some of the responses hidden in the different agendas lead to? Were the agendas you heard the same as or different than your own listening agendas?

Do you think the speakers felt really "heard"?

Did the Listeners' agendas get them what they wanted? Was it a high-quality conversation?

Day 2: Feeding the W.O.L.F.

On a full stomach, we're all better listeners. So during this section, we'll look at 3 ways one can keep ones hungers fed. This is where the coach will be helping their clients. Think about one of your personal hungers for a moment, and hold it in mind as you read through the options below. There are three main ways to feed a hungry WOLF.

1. Acknowledge where it's already being fed.

Many of us are like the blind man who starved to death at a banquet. There was food all around him but he didn't know it was there. It's time to start noticing where the food is in your life. How many places in your life are you already getting exactly what you hunger for? Who or what is already helping to satisfy that need? Do you ever brush off compliments or ignore people when they acknowledge you? How could you start letting those acknowledgments in? And on the rare occasions when your hunger *is* fed, do you spend any time enjoying the sensation? Sometimes, what we've been so urgently seeking is right there in front of us. We just need to open our eyes and take the time to enjoy it.

2. Set up a feeding schedule.

If what you are hungering for isn't right in frcnt of you, it's time to start creating it. There are two ways to do this. First, you can set aside time to feed the hunger yourself. If you hunger to be "right," you might make a list of 10 ways you were "right" during the week. Then smile and acknowledge yourself for it, basking in the glory of your "rightness" for a minute or two. If your hunger is to be appreciated, you could spend a few minutes at the end of each day appreciating all the wonderful things you did, and the amazing person that you already are. You can also imagine other people giving you exactly what you want and need, and revel in how very good it feels.

Second, you can ask other people to help feed your hunger. Let your supportive friends know when you need a hug, a pep talk, or a pat on the back. One coach gave self-addressed postcards to all her friends and asked them to send her one each week, with a short note about what they liked about her. Another asked his wife to tell him 3 things he had done *right* each week. Does this seem silly or selfish? Then look at it this way: You actually help other people fill their own hunger to contribute by allowing them to contribute to you. It's a win-win game.

Third, feed the people around you. This is going to be one of the more effective ways a client can be using the "external means of feeding their hunger. The following is a message that could be delivered to a client as well as looked at for the coach to maintain a hunger satisfied coaching space

"If there's not a wealth of supportive people around you, then it's time to prime the pump." By taking some simple daily actions you can create a support structure that will nourish you every day of our life. (And if you *do* have a strong support network, you'll recognize this as an excellent way to keep it strong and healthy.)

Start giving to other people, what you most want to receive yourself. If you hunger for appreciation, then appreciate 3 other people each day. Feel the joy of that appreciation. If you hunger for power, start delegating power to the people you manage and watch how it expands your own influence. If you hunger to be understood, take the time to truly listen and understand someone close to you. By giving what you most want to receive, you very often receive it in return. It's like smiling at a stranger and having them smile back. Smiles (and support) need to start somewhere and you're the best source—because you're the *only* source that you have the power to change."

When you accept your own hungers, and lovingly allow yourself to get them fed, your ability to listen expands tremendously. You can let go of your old listening agendas, and truly hear what your clients are saying. It's a remarkable gift, for them and for you.

More Practice Time

Three Hungers that affect my listening are:

1. _____
2. _____
3. _____

Three new ways I can feed each hunger are:

Hunger #1

a. _____

b. _____

c. _____

Hunger #2

a. _____

b. _____

c. _____

Hunger #3

a. _____

b. _____

c. _____

Exercise

1. Think of giving 3 people what you most Hunger for. Have all 3 be from a different category, such as: One it would be hard to give to, one it would be easy to give to, and one it would be neutral to give to; or from different areas such as my work, my family, my community. Then write a few notes about how it would feel to do so.

a. _____

_____

b. _____

_____

c. _____

_____

2. List 3 places where you're actually getting your Hunger met already. Then add a sentence or two about how it feels to have the Hunger met this way.

a. _____

_____

b. _____

_____

c. _____

_____

3. Feed the Hunger yourself. Come up with 3 fulfilling, unique, satisfying, zany, comforting, nurturing or even wild and outrageous ways to fill the Hunger yourself — either on your own, or by enlisting the aid of others. What will you do? How will it feel?

a. _____

_____

b. _____

_____

c. _____

_____

Day 3: Listen to Yourself

We talk to ourselves all day long. Whether we realize it or not, there's a constant inner dialogue going on inside our head. For example, a second ago you may have said to yourself "Yes, that's true. I talk to myself constantly," or "Not me, I never talk to myself." Either way, you were carrying on a a little chat with yourself. That inner voice is always with us, every waking moment. And the quality of what it says makes a significant difference in our lives.

"If the voice inside your head were a person, would you want to be its friend?"

Is your Inner Voice a wise counsellor who you can turn to for advice, or a harsh critic who condemns you for every move you make? For most of us, it's somewhere in between, and it probably varies according to the situation that we're in. Since our inner dialogue is primarily subconscious, it takes a little creative effort to discover what we're saying to ourselves...and what we're listening for.

What are some things that people might listen to themselves for? What are the common patterns or threads?

_____

_____

_____

_____

How does our agenda change in response to different people or situations? What are some examples of this?

_____

_____

_____

How does our state of Hunger affect the way we talk to ourselves? How does that change our ability to listen to ourselves?

_____

_____

If the voice(s) in your head were a character from a movie, who would it be?

_____

_____

What value does this character have to offer?

_____

_____

How could this character help you be a better coach?

_____

_____

_____

Exercise:

Immerse yourself in the experience of something that regularly impacts you (involving such topics as money, relationships, food, health, adventure, career, learning, risk, or technology...to name just a few) and become aware of your inner dialogue.

Listen to what you say to yourself. Do you have an agenda when you're listening? What presuppositions might you have?

> **Coaching Tip:**
> While we know that listening without an agenda is inherently an agenda, what we're really after is as clean a state of listening as is possible. So, let go of the assumptions, let go of what you think you know and be willing to ride the roller coaster of the unknown that is your client.

When you listen, do you hear permission or denial? Encouragement or criticism? Understanding and love, judgment and justification? What happens when you shift your agenda? Practice listening without agenda.

Just hear what's there. How was it different? What did you hear that you might not have heard before?

Day 4: Taming Your Wolf

Knowing the nature of our own personal WOLF makes it easier to tame the beast. Once we know that we're listening to fill the Hunger to "be right" we can look for ways to be right outside of the coaching situation. We can also give ourselves permission to let the client be right while we're on the call. In essence, we create a situation where everyone wins.

When we listen to the voice inside our own head, we discover how to listen more effectively to the voices in our clients' heads. We can hear their personal agendas and unveil the

Hungers that drive their actions. Yet ultimately, it's the intention behind our listening that makes the crucial difference in our client's lives. When we listen for their Hungers, why are we listening? Is it to "fix" them? Or to accept them? Is it to show how brilliant we are as coaches? Or to allow the client to see what an opportunity he has to enrich his life? Our intention shapes the reason behind everything we do as a coach.

So when we talk about what a coach listens for…it's not really the content that we're talking about. It's the intent behind the listening. With that in mind, a coach simply listens for what's there, with the intent of reflecting honestly and respectfully back to the client what she hears. It's called "listening without an agenda," and it's the purest form of coaching that there is. As we listen without an agenda, some things will naturally start to stand out.

What types of things does a coach tend to hear?

_____

_____

_____

How can your own natural listening agenda help you listen without an agenda? How could this make you a better coach?

_____

_____

_____

_____

Now that your listening is attuned. We'll go or. to the types of questions and how they are used. If you feel the need for a break, now would be a good time.

The River of Questions

Questions like rivers have all sorts of features. Some parts of the river are smooth, some are rough. Some have sandy bottoms and some are muck and mire. And some riverbanks have trees and branches sticking out, and some are full of rocks. The next section is about exploring the river of questions. There are the deep flowing areas of open-ended questions, and the stopping points of closed end questions. The are the murky parts of queggestions and the rapids of Danger Will Robinson. Lastly, there is the smooth easy drift of the Socratic question types. All questions are not the same. They are not designed to be. There are all different types of questions, however for the purpose of this material I'll be covering only four parts of this river.*

    a. Open-ended/Closed-end questions
    b. Queggestions
    c. "Danger Will Robinson" questions
    d. Socrates Breakdown of six essential kinds.

*Socratic Questions have six categories already built in.

Riversection 1. Open-Ended and Closed End Questions

Open-ended questions are often called "Discovery" questions by most coaches. One of the key places a coach works with a client is to help them discover (uncover) what they don't know they know. These are also called "Possibility" Questions since they open up new ideas, vistas and options.

Open-ended questions are simple to describe, these are "essay" answer questions...something that can't be answered by a mere yes or no, or a single data point of information...Many of these questions invoke discovery, reflection, or a looking deeper.

A good discovery question will often have the client ruminate on the answer, mulling about possibilities, areas of exploration and options they hadn't considered before. It is a door opener to some deeper, broader, or more comprehensive grasp of the topic at hand and its relationship to the client.

"Truth dwells in the deeps" Schiller

Discovery questions essentially "uncover," that which is hidden, unconsciously known but not accessed. It is like shining a light into the corners of your attic, basement or even turning your telescope to the sky and seeing what's out there.

Discovery questions are also not some things.

These are not questions that lead the client to an answer the coach thinks they should have. If used like that, we give up to role of coach for mother, lawyer, employer, or some other authority figure who wants us to behave in a particular way that suits them.

In a court of law, this is called leading the witness. When we lead the client where we think they need to go, we are very subtly putting our fingerprints on their hands. There is a subliminal message given in this way that says, "You don't know where you need to go but I do, so I'll lead you to the solution but you'll think it's yours."

Sometimes one may think they are asking an open-ended question, and just because someone responds with more than a yes/no, it seems to confirm that they did, indeed, ask one. This is not always true. There's an assumption hidden in the pseudo discovery question. The assumption is that the client will not just say yes or no.

Let's take an example. When asked the following question, some people might respond with a number of ideas.

"Do you know what you might do to handle that issue?"

On the surface it seems to prompt some deeper thinking, however often the coach would be startled if the client simply replied. "No, I don't." Which is a perfectly legitimate answer to a "Do you…question.

The coach then might fumble around to come up with a question in response to the answer the coach wasn't expecting. In this moment of being off balance, often the coach will shift gears and track down their internal list of "great questions" that they've collected in their memory and come up with a formulaic rejoinder to the client something along the lines of, "Well, if you did know, what would it be?" There are times when this works. The danger of any question's momentary effectiveness is the potential for the question to become a formula.

Whenever I hear this question ("And if you did know what would that be?") in a class or in an observed coaching my soul wants to cry out, "I AM NOT A FORMULA!" and my response to being the imaginary client in that moment is to reply to the coach, "Well, if you could ask a non-formulaic question what would it be?" In my imagining, there are some people who would be severely offended by my response. Some would find it amusing, and some would just get the point. The point is simply:

Custom-create your questions to the client in the moment and drop the formulas.

Clearly, the game of asking open-ended questions requires some practice so that we can become accustomed to having these questions be drawn out of us in any specific moment. Yes, I said the question is drawn out of us. What I mean there is this. We are in service to the client, to be used by them as they advance in life toward their solutions, goals, dreams or visions. To that end, it is useful to be well trained enough so that in any given moment, whatever question the client needs us to ask, is drawn out of us like the client raising water from the well.

This kind of being in service interaction can only occur when we are in a good connected relationship with our client. When we are not, the dynamic is relegated to one of the coach doing it to the client.

For us, it is like being a masterful musician in our client's orchestra. They as the conductor need us to give a virtuoso performance in whatever music they require of us when called to in their personal symphony. If it is a deep question, then we need to be able to play it. If it is a pointed, focused or linear question, then we need to be able to play that. Whatever notes of questions they require are what we need to be skilled enough, egoless enough, and in tune enough to bring out when beckoned.

Let's play a game. On the next page you will find two triangles. One will be for open-ended beginnings of questions and the other will be for closed-end questions. In between, will be a group of question beginnings. Take the question beginnings out of the circle and place them in the appropriate box.

If you have any questions about the accuracy of your responses then there's a diagram in the very back of the book with a view for you.

Have a good time.

Open-Ended Questions

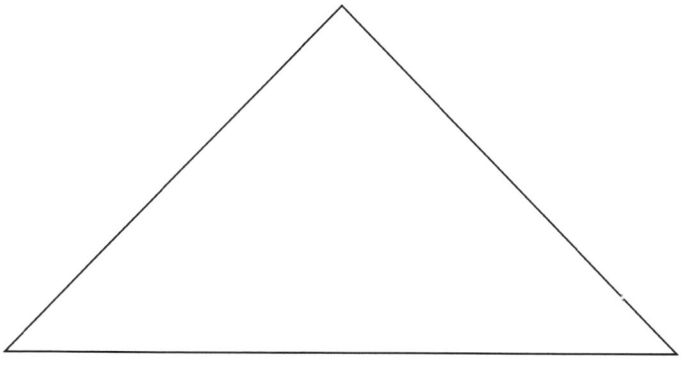

Do you think…? Can you…?
What if…? How would you…? Is
there…? What would happen…?
When will? Where can you…?
What do you think…? Are
you…? If you could would
you…? Under what
circumstances would you…?

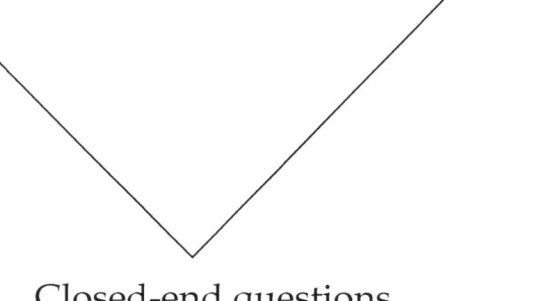

Closed-end questions

Here are some discovery questions for you, now that you have completed the exercise. (do see the built in assumption in my statement)?

What did you notice about your ability to discern the two?

What will help you grow your ability to generate true discovery questions more naturally?

If you checked the back of the book, and disagreed with some of the answers, what was at the heart of your disagreement?

In your mind, what is the difference between a deep discovery question and a discovery 'lite' question?

Riversection 2. Queggestions

Queggestions are suggestions masquerading as a question. Often queggestions are placed in the group of discovery questions mistakenly. One usually finds them under the guise of "what if?" i.e. "What if you went into your bosses office and discussed his propensity for stepping all over your boundaries? What would happen then?" Embedded in the question of what if, is the suggestion that this is something the client should do, or consider doing. And while there may be the mystery of not knowing what will happen, it leads the client to an action of the coaches choosing instead of the client's creation.

This doesn't make the queggestions bad questions, it is simply that they are more about the coach than about the client. It's the coach's job to have the session be about the client's wisdom instead of their own. Here are some more examples that while they have value, are leading to a specific direction. Queggestions are very useful in training.

If you were going to replace queggestions with something what would you replace them with?

What personal needs might be causing you to create queggestions?

What image of yourself as a coach would you have to relinquish in order to use queggestions less?

Riversection 3. "Danger Will Robinson"

During the 60's there was a television show called Lost in Space. The plot line of the show was based around a number of space travelers (a family called the Robinsons) who had gone off course through some cataclysmic event and were now spending the next four or five years of television programming desperately trying to return home.

In the cast, there was a robot character that watched out for the youngest little boy. Whenever it looked like the robot's sensors picked up a threat the robot spoke, "Danger Will Robinson, danger..."

Lost in Space is an appropriate metaphor for the coach seeking to move toward mastery of questions as a primary skill set. For whenever the coach lurches off course into a particular agenda they would be well served by their own internal guide speaking, "Danger Will Robinson...Danger." This might prevent them from being lost in an undesirable space that a particular question creates.

On the next page are some of the hazards a coach might inadvertently encounter on their way to their coaching mastery. Hopefully the mere listing by me, and review by you will be sufficient to set up your own early warning system. If not, I'm certain you can count on your client to alert you to the consequences of one of these items. It may however, be too late once they have.

1.   **Interrogation** - no one likes to feel they are being backed into a corner and repeatedly asked for details i.e. "Where were you on the 29th of May? While it may look supportive, the coach needs to be sensitive to whether they are backing the client into a corner of no viable choice.

2.   **Pigeonholing** - these questions are about a predetermined judgment by the coach, looking for validation of a particular assessment/assumption. No one enjoys being stereotyped by someone who is allegedly there to help him. People are unique. i.e. "What do you sales types typically do in that situation?"

3.   **Confronting** - continually asking "why?" will put someone on the defensive, how do you feel when that is done to you? "When are you going to finally take responsibility for your life?" If spoken in a challenging tone in some leftover transformational workshop attempt to break someone through, it can well backfire and completely break the trust level of the client. No client needs another policeman in their life. Especially not if they are paying for it.

4.   **"Leading the witness"** - these kinds of questions are about the "answer" the coach has and wants the client to get, the potential here is the condescension that, "I the coach have the answer and you the child must be led to it." Often the client will sense it and ask, "What is it you want me to get to? What is it you want me to see/understand?" Or simply state "It seems like you have an answer you're not telling me."

5.   **Accusing** - the potential damage of this kind of question is obvious. i.e. "Why did you do that?"

6.   **Impugning** - an aggressive disbelieving, calling the person a liar type of question. If you are looking for the veracity of a particular statement there are many ways to get

to that without attacking the client. i.e. "You don't expect me to believe that?"

7. **What if** – These are possibility questions; the kind that help a client envision something they want in particular detail or something they want to accomplish and perhaps thought was not possible. It's important to note here that while "what if?" is a very powerful tool of possibility, it can also send a client into the land of disempowerment, worry, and fear. Depending on someone's conditioning or emotional state, the 'what if' question could generate 'What if something goes wrong?' or 'What if I can't make enough money?' Then the 'what if' question has become a liability.

On the other hand, there is the potential for the "what if" question to be a reality checker, a grounding question, and a rule challenge as well as a possibility generator. It's all related to the context, timing and situation in which the question is posed. This is part of what keeps masterful questions a living art instead of merely a science. There is no definitive, all the time answer for what question goes where and when.

Many of these 'what if' questions are born out of the curiosity about who the client really is, what's really going on instead of merely what's stated, and where does the client really want to go.

8. **Why** - When asked from a place of genuine curiosity, in much the same way as a child, they are very useful. When asked in a confronting or challenging tone and manner, you can guarantee that the client will go on the defensive. "Why would you possibly want to do that?

For Danger Will Robinson Questions 9 and 10, I ask you this. What have you found to be the most impractical, annoying, useless, unsettling, and downright destructive question types? Pick your favorite two and write them in for the 9 and 10 spot. Then write an example of the question below your pick.

9. _____

_____

_____

_____

_____

_____

10. _____

_____

_____

_____

_____

_____

The Village of Socrates

In the days of the ancient Greeks, the philosophers practiced the Socratic method for discovering truth and knowledge. The way they believed to get to the truth was by asking questions of a person. They believed the person already held the truth within their heart but needed to become aware of what he already knew. The questions would be a source to help the student turn inward to discover himself. One of the best, most simple questions is, *"What do you want?*

Questions are then the basis for coaches to help their clients get to where they really want to go, as well as for helping your them uncover their own truths.

The Socratic method is simply a way of asking questions that permits the answerer to develop her/his own point of view. It is intended to be helpful, but it can feel like being put on the spot unless the questions are very easy. An example of an easy question is, "What is the worst experience you have had in buying these products in the past?" (An example of a hard question is "What would it take for you to buy from me today?" asked in the first 2 minutes of the sales meeting.

Due to the rapid addition of new information and the advancement of science and technology that occur almost daily, a coach must constantly expand his or her horizons beyond simple gathering information and relying problem solving principles.

It is imperative that coaches help foster critical thinking. Critical thinking is the process we use to reflect on, access and judge the assumptions beneath our own and others ideas and actions.

Socratic questioning is at the heart of critical thinking, the following lists, illuminate the six types of Socratic questions. Take some time to study how they're built.

Questions for Clarification, or that Probe Conceptual understandings

What do you mean by _____?

What is your main point?

How does _____ relate to _____?

Would you put that another way?

Is your basic point _____ or _____?

What do you think is the main issue here?

Which do you mean _____ or _____?

How does this relate to your problem, discussion, or issue?

Will you explain that further?

Would you say more about that?

What makes you say that?

Questions that Probe Assumptions

What are you assuming?

What could we assume instead?

You seem to be assuming _____. Do I understand you correctly?

What has you base your reasoning on _____ instead of _____?

Is that always the case? What makes the assumption holds here?

How can you verify or disprove that assumption?

What Would happen if...?

What If it wasn't that way?

What are you assuming?

What assumptions would be useful to employ here?

What if there were no assumptions, how would that change how you saw this situation?

What's the upside or downside of following that assumption?

What else might be going on?

Questions that Probe Reasons and Evidence for a position

What would be an example?

What are your reasons for saying that?

What other information do you need?

What led you to that belief?

How does that apply to this case?

What would change your mind?

Who is in a position to know that is true?

How could we find out if that is true?

What is the true nature of this?

What makes this keep happening?

What has to happen for you to be sure?

What do you think causes...?

What's at the core of that?

How will you know when you've attained that?

What will you need to know along the way that will prove you're on the right course?

Questions about Viewpoints or Perspectives

If that happened, what else would happen as a result?

What effect would that have?

Would that necessarily happen or only probably happen?

If _____ and _____ are the case, then what might also be true?

What would be an alternative?

What's another way to look at it?

Who benefits?

What are the strengths and weaknesses of...?

What is the difference between... and...?

How are...and ...similar?

What makes you chose this perspective over others?

How many other perspectives can you imagine?

How would _____see that differently?

Questions that Probe Implications or Consequences of a position.

What generalizations can you make?

What are the consequences of that assumption?

How could...be used to...?

What are the implications of...?

How does...affect...?

How does...tie in with what you've learned before?

What makes... important?
What is the best... and why?

What else might happen as a result?

What effect would that have?

Would that necessarily happen or only probably happen?

If this and this is the case, then what else must also be true?

Would any implication or result cause you to think differently?

Questions about the Question

How can we find out?

What does this question assume?

Would _____ ask this question differently?

How could someone settle this question?

Can we break this question down at all?

Is this question easy or hard to answer? Why?

Does this question ask us to evaluate something? What?

Do we both agree that this is the question?

To answer this question, what other questions must we answer first?

How would _____ state the issue?

What makes this issue important?

Is this the most important question, or is there an underlying question that is really the issue?

What does...mean?

What would make this question more powerful for you?

The Quicksand of Expertise

One of the bigger challenges for a coach hinges on the value of their expertise. As a coach, you have gathered much information, experience and practice in a number of realms. In fact, you may have been at a particular subject for many, many years. While the province of the coach is not to give advice, there are still ways in which the expertise you have worked so hard for will be useful.

The cleanest way to use your expertise is to have it inform your questions. You still won't be leading them to your answer, however, you will be employing questions in an area someone else might not even consider asking unless they have your same expertise.

Here's an example of how the experience can inform the question.

I have a lot of years practice, training, and study in the area of presentations. There are many things that I've come in contact with which will make a persons public speaking, or presenting, much more engaging. In fact I could write about on all the how to's of it. However, when I'm coaching someone on presentation the game is different, and I look to have the client answer some questions in their own way.

One of the things I know about effective presenting is how important it is to have the participants walk away with something they can immediately apply in a practical way. This is part of anchoring the experience for them. A question I might ask a client would be, "What is it you're looking for them to be able to do as a result of having spent this time with you?" As you can see, while my knowledge of the presenting game is present by knowing which question to ask, I have neither led them to an answer I think they should have, nor told them that what they must do is have them make the audience feel a particular way. The key on the coach's end is to relinquish any need to have them agree with you on what the outcome will be. That way you can continue to coach toward endorsing and strengthening your clients connection to their own inner wisdom.

If you as the coach have expertise in an area and are "mentoring" the client or team, then of course you will impart your expertise of how a particular task can be easily completed. In the coaching relationship, you may also give the client or team members the option to explore other ways to complete the task.

Many individuals, such as busy entrepreneurs, hire coaches to help them keep focused and not get overwhelmed. Many corporations will hire coaches to get an outsider's input and expertise. And in working with individuals at any level, we all desire the same things…healthy relationships, recognition for doing a great job, a rewarding career and enough money to allow us to live the lifestyle we desire.

On the next page are some observations that might be helpful to remember as you consider giving advice.

- Often the pivotal question is more powerful than individual instruction.

- Always try to ask a question of your client before giving advice.

- Much deeper understanding comes from the client if he is first asked to think of the answer to the question.

- Creativity is stimulated better by asking questions.

- The coach will learn more by asking than by telling.

- When trying to solve your own problem, find the right person to ask you the right questions.

Below is the bottom line on advice:

"Information and Expertise have a shelf life, discovery is eternal."

The Uncharted Territory of The Unanswered Question™

Over the course of many coaching sessions, the coach will begin to hear in the background, something nagging at the edge of their consciousness. It will be something that seems to be drawing attention like a gnat buzzing far away....

Each one of us, and each of our clients has within, an "Unanswered Question" that has been present since childhood. Most all of the activities in one's life have been subtly, and sometimes not so, designed to provide us with an opportunity to experience or receive the answer to this question. The goals, visions, ventures and escapades have drawn us from one moment to another. They have behind them something that is so fundamental, so critical, that much of our lives is devoted to the search. It feels like our own personal "Grail." It is related to self-definition and as such requires an answer.

As our clients progress from having "a life I don't want," to "a life I do want," there is the sense of something more - something intrinsically important and dancing at the shadows of awareness with an imperative that eventually begins to surface.

The power of the unanswered question is pervasive and until it's answered it is difficult, although not impossible, for our clients to truly "relax" and be at peace with themselves. It is also difficult, though not impossible for them to truly entertain the question: "Now that my life is working, what do I want it to be about?" This is a question that cannot be genuinely asked while ones internal hungers, and external needs are at stake. It can only be truly asked when there is no need working, and no hunger driving. Hungers will always be present, however, it's the degree to which it has seemingly disappeared that is being addressed.

Answering this question will ease the path of connection to one's LifeWork. There is a large distinction to be drawn between the work/activity one is doing in ones life, and one's LifeWork. One's LifeWork is that which one is "here to do." It is what one has been trained for, gifted for, led to, spiritually designed for, and it requires one's full capability in order to have it be done easily. When we are distracted by our unanswered question, we are not nearly as free to give our full attention to this work. In addition, many clients will substitute busyness and the seemingness of working hard to replace the depth of satisfaction and fulfillment that comes from engaging with one's LifeWork

The main challenge then is to discover "what's really going on in this picture." With yourself, and with your clients, it will demand asking some deep and hard questions at times. It may be elusive, and it may feel like it's been answered, however the coach's true job could be characterized by this "higher" work and it might well be considered that the other work a coach does with a client is merely, "getting ready" for the real possibilities of what their clients' lives can be about.

An example of this question is here in my own life. At some point, I realized I had always been asking, "Will I be wanted for who I am and what I do in the world, Will I be wanted for just me?" As I reviewed my life, this question had permeated all my activities. It had defined my life with its imperative. It wasn't until a I was standing in front of a packed room at an International Coach Federation conference that I got it answered.

I had just presented a topic that was expressly me. I had done it in a style that used all of my creativity, passion, skills, intelligence, being and things that I love in my life. My wit, compassion and desire for people to have something of value that had been generated from deep inside my had been accepted. The room was giving me a standing ovation, cheering and whistling. I had arrived.

The final element that brought it home to me came from my coach who had coached me for 9 years, and known me for 17. At the back of the room, as the people were shuffling out, he said to me, "That was ALL you. There was no apology, no approval seeking, no looking to please or impress, no "becoming" it was simply YOU."

In that moment, I felt an enormous release. It was if something that had been hanging over my head for over 40 years had finally disappeared. I had gotten my answer, and the answer was a resounding YES! Yes, I was wanted for me, yes, I was wanted for my work, YES.

It was not surprising to me that my contribution in the world began to crystallize in a much different fashion. Now I could get on with it. I could work on what I was built for. I could use all of the years of experiences, training, practice, knowledge, fumblings and succeedings, intelligence, creativity, and heart to bring forth what I had in me without needing others to okay it. I was finally free to fulfill my design.

So I invite you to engage in this question for yourself and for your clients. It's both a listening for and an inquiry. Not all of your clients will be ready to evoke this kind of recognition. Not all of your clients will be interested. You yourself may not be interested. If you are though, I urge you to get your life working the way you want it to so that you can ask it from a clear space.

The next few pages have some questions for you, and for your clients. The idea here is not to answer glibly and quickly for this is the stuff of meaning, of existence and as such deserves the respect of matters with that level of importance. While the questions may seem to ask obvious things, they are designed to lead through a process of deepening awareness. They are designed to plant seeds in the fertile soil of the soul. Give yourself some quiet time, some genuinely "you" time. Set yourself up to have all other priorities fade into the background while you are looking at these questions.

1. What were all the jobs and roles that figured large in your life (either in significance, or in length)?

2. What jobs and roles have you've played, and what questions were answered about you to yourself by your participation in each of them?

3. What is your personal philosophy about how the world should be, in its ideal condition? What would need to happen in order for it to get there?

4. What were the primary moments and places where you were "a public figure," or where you spoke out in public advocating something, or spoke out about something? What were you really saying as part of your public presence?

5. What is it you believe that people need to have, do, or be, in order to be well in the world and why is it important to you that it be that way?

6. What is it that you must know about YOU? If you finally knew it, it would allow you to just relax and simply get on with your life with no further energy expended this item? What is your defining Unanswered Question?

7. What MUST happen in order for you to get this answered truly and deeply, for all time, and resonating to all corners of your being?

The Mines of Question Design

Every question is designed to do a specific thing. It could be to gather information, it could be to probe, challenge or help the client reflect. It could be to stretch, or shift the client's perspective. It could be to help them tap into the core of their being or challenge their self-perception. It might even simply be designed to generate action and have them take supported concrete steps toward a goal. In any event, all questions have a design in them. Here's your chance on the next few pages to examine some questions and see what they are designed to do.

By looking at how they are built, you'll grasp a keener sense in your own ability to construct them yourself. Deconstructing questions is a much more potent path toward mastery than simply repeating them from rote, or reading them from a list. The understanding goes much deeper when you take the time to figure out exactly how the question does what it does.

My strong recommendation is that you spend some time here. This can raise the base line level of your question artistry overnight.

There are about three and a half pages to play with. You can try them all at once, or take them in bite-size chunks. What makes it good question? What makes it a bad one? Where is the question designed to reach? What outcome is the question looking for? The question is, what manner of using this exercise will serve you best?

What the Question is	What the question is designed to do
What is something you know you need to start (or stop) doing differently, the doing of which would start a beneficial chain of events?	
What do you need to do to create balance?	
How would you feel if you had a plan?	
What would that plan look like?	
How would you find ways to put your plan in action?	
What do you already know?	
What will you accomplish that you will feel good about at the end of the day?	
What do you want and what do the people you care about want?	
What kind of person do you need to be to achieve your goals?	
What prevents you from having the right to what you want, now?	
What will get you there?	

What will happen if you don't achieve your goals? If you do?	
What will it take for you to stop struggling?	
What do you need to do to create balance?	
What would be enough money (love, security, peace) for you?	
How would you find ways to put your plan in action?	
What do you already know?	
What would it take.....	
What two actions would it take?	
How would it feel not to be moody?	
What is it that you do that makes you feel good about yourself?	
If you were a coach listening to this what would you say?	
If there were a way for you to get what you really want - faster, with less effort, and with integrity, would you be willing to give it a shot?	

What is the biggest obstacle you face right now in your career or personal life, and how can you use it to your advantage?	
What would it take to get you to your next level of success? What keeps you from going there?	
What is the one thing, that if practiced consistently, would make the most impact in your life?	
Is your business working for you or are you working for your business?	
How do you think someone could support you in getting that?	
What are you carrying around in your backpack that you don't need?	
What would it feel like to not suffer?	
What would you lose by not suffering?	
How does it feel to be fair? Honest?	
What are you excited about today?	
What are you proud about this week?	

What will you accomplish that you will feel good about at the end of the day?	

Well, what did you learn? Now that you've spent some time with the full range of questions, what creates them, how they are designed, what gets in their way and what else is possible with them, where have you brought yourself? What new air will you breathe? What will you do with what you've learned and how will you make it real for you? What new questions are opened up for you as part of the process?

You see, the cool deal about engaging with questions and being curious, is that they open up more questions. Besides, answers are all over the place.

About the author

Michael Stratford

PO Box 3482
Laguna Hills, CA 92654

949-716-9267
yokoach@aol.com
www.creativeu.com

There are 2 ways to know Michael – professionally and personally.

First, in the coaching profession: Michael was an early adopter of professional coaching, and by early 1999, he had already been awarded the prestigious ICF Master Certified Coach designation. Among his first clients in 1995 was a lead singer in a rock band, and he soon earned a reputation as the 'Rock Band Coach', helping 15 bands achieve a level of excellence in communication and team performance, that led him to coach some of the top Fortune 50 executives in personal and team performance.

Using leading edge teleclass technology, Michael has trained thousands of coaches worldwide. He's worked for 3 different Coach Training Schools, in person training for The Coaches Certification Institute. He has developed coach training curriculum for many of these organizations, as well as designing an in-house Manager-to-Coach Training Program used in corporations. A prolific and published author, Michael has also written children's stories, Haiku, Plays produced off-Broadway, a soon to be released "The Game of Coaching," The Master Coach Series Vol. 1-3, and a chapter in "Achieving Extraordinary Success as a Coach.

Michael is an engaging and articulate presenter, who will have you laughing while you learn. He has given presentations internationally on topics including Irresistible Attraction, Compelling Presentations, The Game of Masterful Questions, Passion, Power and Communication, The Creativity Connection, The Game of Your Life, The Game of Your Business and his favorite topic, Playing Your Way to a Great Life.

Michael has a light and playful approach, yet through his masterful coaching and training, he quickly reveals a depth of knowledge and understanding on a wide range of human and organizational issues.

The second way to know Michael is as "regular guy". Michael has had over 56 different jobs (he counted), and four careers (including Coaching, Actor/Director on Broadway and TV, VP of Operations for PSA/USA, and a General Contractor in Manhattan).

Much of his learning and love of Play was rekindled through interacting with his son Matthew. His latest adventures include: being delightfully newly married to a wonderful Aussie Coach named Carly, who is his "A to Z and then some," moving to California where snow is a choice, and, having the most fun he's ever had, launching his "Game Of... Play your Way to Success" series of books, tapes, workshops, on topics such as The Game of Your Life, The Game of Your Business, The Game of Leadership, The Game of Money, and The Game of Relationship. You get the picture. Yes, he's "Chicken Souping" it.

Request, Offer and Shameless piece of Promotion

Let Me Know how to serve you.

Request

First, I'd like some feedback about how this material affected you. What was your experience in reading it through? What, if anything would have helped you understand it easier? What, if anything would have made it more practical? My request is for feedback that doesn't contain what you think I should do, but rather, what happened for you. If I get enough of a similar piece of feedback, trust me, I'll make course corrections to make this book more useful. Of course I'll do it in my own style (I know you wouldn't want it any other way).

Offer

I'm looking for reports of how this material is being used by coaches and their clients to help them along in their journey. If you send me some brief stories (five to ten lines is good) then I will collect them and publish a number of them in my next printing at the back of this book. Since the printings are on demand, and the first printing was a small run, it's likely that they will be printed again by end of 2004.

I will let you know if your story is selected, and when the likely printing will be. My request is that you work with the ideas for a while, maybe 3 months or so, in order to get a feel for how it all works together. Let me know what happened. Include the date you started working with it and how long you kept attention on it. If it's a client's story, please keep the name confidential and refer to them as "a client I worked with." I'm interested to learn what people are doing with what I've written. How are you using it? What new creative ways have you come up with to maximize the communication, and value of these ideas. Who knows, I may just publish a full book of collected stories, with 25% of the profit to a charity.

Please send all stories or feedback to:

michaelstratford@michaelstratford.com

Shameless Piece of Promotion

This material can also be delivered in a workshop, keynote, or a teleclass. If you, your group, or your organization would like me to fulfil any of those three, please give me a call or send me an email. I'd be happy to help you take this work further.

The live presentation of this material has a lot of fun, cool, and sometimes profound exercises. They really bring the material home in a visceral way.

The teleclass is fun, challenging, and has the convenience of being able to take it while in your shorts. You might also be able to join in and take a teleclass on your own when I offer one.

So, let me know what works for you.

michaelstratford@michaelstratford.com

The client is unique.
The client is intelligent.
The client is capable.
The client knows how to solve problems.
The client is responsible for his/her own life.
The client is an adult.
The client is personally accountable.
The client is imaginative.
The client is creative.
The client is courageous.
The client knows how to follow through.
The client has his/her own sense of order and organizing principles.
The client has a unique dream/vision or goal.
The client has strengths, talents, and skills.
The client knows how to accomplish.
The client has or can get what they need.
The client knows how to learn.
The client is whole.
The client knows how to be clear.
The client is resilient.
The client is competent in the world.
The client can provide for himself.
The client knows how to focus.
The client has her own values and principles.
The client has his own inner compass.
The client is strong.

My answer is simple. Seeing my clients this way allows me to coach respectfully, powerfully, and without agenda. It becomes a treasure hunt of who this person is and a marvelous unfolding of how they're uniquely going to get where they want to go. It allows me to serve.

Michael Stratford

Made in the USA
San Bernardino, CA
16 December 2016